The Lord is *My* Inspiration

For God's Nation

Cordell "Cowieyo" Taylor

Xulon Press

Xulon Press
555 Winderley Pl, Suite 225
Maitland, FL 32751
407.339.4217
www.xulonpress.com

© 2024 by Cordell "Cowieyo" Taylor

All rights reserved solely by the author. The author guarantees all contents are original and do not infringe upon the legal rights of any other person or work. No part of this book may be reproduced in any form without the permission of the author.

Due to the changing nature of the Internet, if there are any web addresses, links, or URLs included in this manuscript, these may have been altered and may no longer be accessible. The views and opinions shared in this book belong solely to the author and do not necessarily reflect those of the publisher. The publisher therefore disclaims responsibility for the views or opinions expressed within the work.

Paperback ISBN-13: 978-1-66289-307-0
Ebook ISBN-13: 978-1-66289-308-7

Love can make you weak or strong.whether you lack it or you belong. Either way you will be singing a love song. Because everyone needs it. And without it you will be spiritually sick. Love can break your heart,into a million parts.Love can lift you high.and the reason why. Love is food for your soul. Or it's like finding a pot of gold. And we all need it to continue down the road.Love sometimes hurt. or can make you feel like some dirt. However that's how it sometimes works. We at times misunderstand what love really is. Because at times it will leave us feeling pissed. Love, real love? Is happy, sad, good, bad, mad, glad or wishing that you had. It's an emotion,also love is devotion. But most of all,I believe it's a sacrifice. From your life. And at times it doesnt feel nice. Love is giving. So keep giving as long as you living.so sow good and loving things. And patiently wait for the goodness it will bring. Give love away each and every day. Then others will have only good things to say. Oh, and by the way, love is the key to life in eternity for you and me. So keep loving as long as you live. regardless how it makes you feel. Because love will heal. For love is alive and real!..

Be careful because the devil is on the prowl, Please don't let him take you down. To Hell deep underground. Don't fall for his tricks, because he's so slick, and we all need to face it. Just look at what he did to Adam and Eve, having them eating the forbidden fruit and Paradise they had to leave. Don't let him do this to you, stopping you from going to heavens of new. Created for me and you. And now you know what to do, Don't be a fool. Just have faith in the Lord, Because why we are living for. To fellowship and worship our creator. is far greater. Than anything or anybody, because he is God Almighty. And he used to visit Adam and Eve, in the cool morning Breeze. And he would do the same in heaven to me and you, can't you see? That God wants us to be in the heavenly's. We were created to praise His holy name, So please don't be ashamed. So stop playing any games. With that evil jealous liar. Because he wants to take you to the Lake of Fire. Please stick with the winners, and stay away from Sinners. Because he's coming back soon. Please people don't let your life be doomed!!

Love is something that is true. Love is loving me and me loving you. Love will make your spirit shine. even those who are spiritually blind. Love is sweet to your soul. transforming you gracefully as you get old. Love will touch your heart. Encouraging you to be strong and smart. Love is giving. so that others have a chance for better living. to help someone with healing. Love brings you blessings. for it's a command from God's Divine lesson. Love is so beautiful. Because it will make you fruitful. loving others is the best thing to do. especially when you say I love you. We all were created out of love. from God Almighty upstairs above. We must preach love all over the world. to every man, woman, boy and girl. because love is in need today. for love is the righteous way. love will give you wisdom words to say. Love will make you smile. because you know that you are God's child.

Lord, I love you so deeply, because you are so unique. And your ways are a mystery, you already know everything that has happened in history. You are the Living God almighty, who made everything and everybody. And I want to thank you for my Lord Jesus Christ, Because he died for my life. So I will give my life to the Lord. Because I hear him knocking at my door, please come to my life today. Because you Jesus Christ is the way here and the truth and the light. Show me how to live right. I believe in you Lord Jesus. Because you love us and want to lead us, to the promised land. Up there with God Almighty in heaven. For that's your plan. And I love you so dearly. Because your love is so sincerely. And I pray that you can hear me. When I say I Will Follow You Jesus. Because I have a million reasons. You are the truth, the light and the way. So I will follow you and pick up my cross everyday. Jesus you are my King. Who rules over everything. And you make my heart sing. Thank you for all that you do. And that's why I deeply do love you.

Don't let the devil and his demons destroy you. Because that's what they're trying to do. We are spiritually blind and we cannot see the battle by spiritual powers for you and me. And we live in a dark world that is losing all of its morals. With boys who want to be girls, and girls who want to be boys. This earth is gloomy with no joy. Some people love to worship the devil, they are digging their own grave with a shovel. But God's people are special, because God created us. In his own image. For we will return to him once we're finished, with the spirit he's given us, when he breathed life in those from the Dust. Don't be blinded by these worldly things, because when you die none of them you can bring. Believe that Jesus is real, so that your trip to Heaven will be sealed. And Don't Stop Believing, and ask him for forgiveness and healing. The world is the Devil's Playground. Just take a good look all around. The world is out of control, people are unkind and cold. It's very blind and so unkind, Honestly? It's a sign of time! It's time to get into a good relationship with our Lord Jesus Christ, stop playing games with your precious life.

My Lord I love you with all of my heart, because you keep it out of the dark. and I love you with all of my mind. Because my Lord you keep me in line. I love you with all of my soul, because with you I will never get old. And I love you with all of my strength, because you are real not a myth. I will pray to you every morning, because I am blessed to see your glory. And I will pray to you at noon, because you keep me in tune. I will pray to you every night, because you are my Guiding Light. That keeps me all right. I will pray to you before I go to bed. Because I know you listen to everything I have said. And I will sing you a song. Because with you is where I want to belong. And I will meditate on your loving ways. And how you have created this day. I will tell others about your love. And how you're looking down from above. I read the Bible no matter what I do. Because it tells me all about you. And I will worship you my Lord Jesus Christ. Because you are the meaning of life. And you treat me so nice. That I look forward to life with you in Paradise.

I have finally found true love. The kind I've been thinking of. The kind that is so true. More deeper than I love you. And so much closer than a wife or a husband. and he holds the world in the palm of his hands. His love is the greatest to exist. and is so precious that I couldn't resist. That I had to be on his list. To enter that unspeakable place. and to finally see my God's Heavenly face. where I can thank him for all his grace. Nothing can compare to his awesome love. Constantly raining from up above. I found his love in my darkest hour. And he comforted me with his mighty power. So I love you more than anything in my life. More than a mother or a child or a wife. Because he is my everything. Who makes my heart sing. Today I'm Walking on Sunshine. 4 his love has got me on Cloud 9. His love I never want to lose. Because if I would, I would be so confused. His love is the foundation of every situation. And I will follow his lead. As I continue to do good deeds. Through all the years he has been right there. Now his voice I can hear. So I will keep on walking this way. Until the day he takes me away. All because I finally found true love today!

We all have to face our demons everyday. Because you can't have life your way. Be prepared for important fight. And training yourself right. So that you can fight with all your might. Cuz these demons won't go away. And they're trained every day. Begin by praying all the time modesty. And to read your Bible constantly. And it's crucial to have faith on your side. Because it's going to be a rough ride. Do not try to hide. Just be strong with victory Pride. Because remember we got God on our side. We have all the weapons we need. So pray in the spirit and take heed. Also when you face your demons it will keep us strong. So that we can carry on. Everybody has to face their demons. Because they hate humans. They are all out to destroy you. So tell me what are you going to do? face all your problems with no fear. Because I have our father is everywhere. And he really does care. So grab that demon by the hair. And tell him to get out of here. Because this is not the the year. And that you are one bad nightmare.

Yes I will praise your name proudly unashamed. how wonderful he is and forever I am all his. Today I live with joy and peace to say the least. Thank you Lord for changing me from that ugly beast. and I thank you for a new heart. made of your hands a precious piece of art. you have made me all brand new. and I thank you Father I truly do love you. I want to thank you for renewing my mind. For you are truthfully one of a kind. I was lost in this world where there's evil. I thank you Lord for snatching Me Up Just Like An Eagle. and put me in the light. where it feels so good and so right. I was blind and I could not see. all you have done for lost soul like me. Lord, I believe in you and your word is true. I love you with all of my heart and mind. Your love I'm truly blessed to find. I thank you for saving a soul like me. because it's your love I do believe. so I gave you my soul. my life with you I will never get old. Lord, you make me feel so brand new. and if I ever lose you I wouldn't know what to do. you are my everything. and that's why I'm constantly calling on your name. and I'm not ashamed. and thank you Lord I'm totally changed.

Sin is not your friend. And I want you to understand. It's all over the land. And I hope that you will comprehend. It's every woman and man. Because we all were born into sin. When Adam and Eve ate the forbidden fruit it began. And life with you will never win. so do your best not to sin. And do not be its fan. Because if you do, then the devil is your friend. And your life will be heading to a dead end. All you need is God's Helping Hand. That's if you want to go to heaven. So start by asking God to forgive you of all your sins. Because when you repent you're born again. And life with God you always win. So it's a must to make God a vital part of your plans. And also to love your fellow woman and man. And to obey all of his commands. So that in heaven he will let you in. also we have the Holy Spirit that God has sent. The help us and give us a helping hand. I'm just trying to remind you that sin is not your friend. Stop doing it before your life comes to an end. And then you won't be able to enter Heaven my friend,

    I've been missing you because you are so true. Now I see that you are important to me. I see you in my dreams. my love together we are a great team. Girl, I need you in my life. I want you more than my wife. Together with you is where I want to be. Together we would be together until eternity. My love come back to me, you are my reality. Baby please understand I want to be your only man. Every night I pray until you come my way. Every single night and day. Only you can make me feel happy, and no more feeling crappy. I want you here in my arms where you can feel all of my charms.be my Valentine. you make me feel so fine. Together in this world I want you to be my girl. Babe there's nothing else to say. So I'll wait until you come my way. Basically day after day. I love you darling can you hear my love calling? It's you that I need. I want to give you my seed. Making something special. Yes indeed. together for eternity .

Faith is the way I live my life today. Putting my trust in Christ. For now and the rest of my life. By faith I dedicate the way I live. To the one I know who's real. the one who possesses all the power to heal. So I would let him drive the wheel. On this journey of my life. As I put my trust in Christ. By faith I Will Follow You Jesus. Because I have so many reasons, my main reason is because you died for my sins. So I want to make amends. You showed me how you're a real friend. For your love I do adore. Thank you for opening up that door. And fighting for me, in this spiritual war. By faith I will pick up my cross no matter the cost. Follow You Jesus Christ. Because your love for me has paid the price. Of all my Sins so you're more than a friend. Whose friendship will never end. I have faith in you. Because you are true. Always showing me the right thing to do. So that I would be all right every day and night. And you make me feel so safe as I continue to hold on to my faith. Fighting a good fight while I follow the light. And I know that it's right. No matter what people say, because you are the truth, the life and the way. So I Will Follow You Lord every single day!

It's love and faith, we need in the human race. and so we all can seek God's Amazing Grace. in this world which is full of disgrace. as we all need to remember our place. especially through these troubled times we all face. remembering to love each other. unconditionally like a child and their mother. Because we all have made mistakes. and I do believe that most of us want to see God's Godly face. Sometimes love hurts so bad. however, loving each other is a command from God our heavenly dad. and when you do love our father will be very glad. so try to love even when you're angry or mad. and if you believe in God faith is a must. because in God we trust. even when our faith is being crushed. just get up and wipe your feet off the dust. Remember what Jesus said? don't be afraid, just believe. Because your faith holds a magic key. and I want to see, That Heaven was made for you and me. And try not to let this world drive you crazy. For we all are God's little babies. even when we're misbehaving.

    It's time for us to pray much more. Because we're in the middle of a spiritual war. And we cannot see. The enemies that we are fighting. They say they are strong and mighty. But so are the Angels in their heavenly bodies. We all need to have a relationship with the Lord Jesus Christ. Because he's the one who could save your life. No one could come to the father except through him. So do right because your life is on a film. Now is the time to follow Jesus Christ. So that your name will be in the book of life. And you will have the right to enter Paradise. But it all starts with you. So tell me what are you going to do. Stay caught up in his worldly life? Just look at what this world has done to Jesus Christ. The only one who did not sin. Tell me who is your friend? I hope that you will understand. Look what this world did to the son of man! Living in this world can make you lose all of your morals. And it can make you sick and blind. And so unkind. So pray with faith on God's level. So that you can defeat that evil devil!

Is a rainy season for me. and I just can't wait to be free. I miss all of my family. and sometimes it messes with my insanity. but I learned to take the bad along with the good. as best as I could. at least I'm still alive. and I must admit I'm one lucky guy. I know that it is not going to rain forever. so just keep going through this rainy season until it gets better. Also it has brought me closer to God. because he consoled me when he heard me sob. This rain has brought me so much pain. and I'm learning how to fight. and I'm learning how to gain. my strength to be strong. so that I could carry on. and when it stops raining I will see the rainbow. and that's when I'll start yelling whoa. It's time for me to glow. and Now I'm a much stronger man. because it's the rainy season. life is not easy and prepare for the storm when life is too breezy. maybe it's good sometimes to go through the rain. because it would give you stress to fight with all the blood through in your veins

I love you in the most delightful way. and I don't care what anyone has to say. I Trust You Lord Jesus Christ. and you are the truth in my life. in every way. you fill me with joy, happiness and ecstasy. My heart has been touched with passionate affections with true Harmony. and I want people to see. what your Mighty love has done to me. because in my heart are emotions when I see you on that tree. And I weep and moan for your love and life you paid the ultimate fee. for a sinner like me. Lord you are the truth and the truth should set us free. and you are the bread of life when I'm hungry. forever I will worship you singing. Glory, glory, glory!! in every opportunity. for my God you are purely holy. and I pray for forgiveness for when I fall down and get dirty. for we all Fall Down because we're earthly. however you die for all of us and say we are all worthy. so please remember that while you're on your journey. Your faith will guide you through all of the Temptations of being earthly. and when you feel unworthy. time to pray to him on your knees. And he will send heavy Angels to you for nursery.

Time is something we have while we're still living on Earth. and it started on our birth. and lots of things have a time limit. but some of us just don't get it. Some of us want things now. and they don't care when or how. but everything is on a time schedule. even those things that are special. We all need time. for our lives to be fine. a time to be born. a time to laugh and a time to mourn. A Time To die and a time for us to cry. a time to say goodbye, a time to plant. A time to say I can't. With so many reasons why. A time to feel. sadly this is real. and a time to heal. when it's pain that you feel. A time to slow down. even regardless of how silly it may sound. a time to build up. and to take out all of your junk. A time to weep. Especially if you think unique. a time to dance. And a time for romance. A time to gain. and there's a time for pain. a time to lose. and it's time to have a fuse. a time to speak. and a time to think. a time of war. and it's time to ask yourself. what Am I living for. Is it for him who can give you peace. or is it for him who would turn you into a wild beast. it's time for you to pick to say the least. Is it in heaven up higher. Or will pick the Lake of Fire. Ask yourself what is your desire?

What becomes of one who has everything but no love in their heart. for love is the Masterpiece of God's will for us all in part. and anyone without love is torn all apart. and for me this is proof that God does exist. and so love is vital to be a child of his. Because love is who God really is. and maybe that's why he said to love even your enemies. because love is a true spiritual remedy. Love is the greatest because love will bring us closer to God. and to love each other is our job. Love is a tense feeling of deep affection. love others and you'll be heading in the right direction. and with God you have a strong connection. for love is a powerful weapon. and at times a misconception. I may not be rich but strive to be rich in love. just like the big man in Heaven up above. and for the simple fact that's what we are made of. Love is the most important commandment. because when you do God's will bless you with so many Investments. so have nothing but love in your heart. because love will keep it away from being dark.

Today. I just want to say. Thank you Lord. for your love and mercy and forgiveness has got me floored.it's indescribable of your loving grace. And I will keep on worth worshiping you in this place. On Earth until we're face to face. As I pray for the entire human race. I love you so plentiful. Because what you have done for me is Unforgettable. How could I not love you? For my heart you healed and renewed. From all the bad times that I've been through. And today I feel brand new. And I do understand things won't always go right. however I will continue to walk to you in the light. And to fight a good fight. Everyday and every night. Because faith is my might. You never gave up on me and now finally I can see. My life with you I would be free. If I just never quit trusting. And then heaven will be a guarantee for me. So I pray today on Bended Knees.To always be the branch on your Mighty tree. And because you are the one who created me. And gave me the right to be who I want to be. And so I choose to follow you. And I just got to say. because you are my Lord Jesus Christ the truth, the life, and the way.

The Lord is My Inspiration

When I was a child, life was a big smile. And as I age I became Wild. And suddenly I was a creature that was so defiled. slowly losing my mind. Walking around so unkind. Because truthfully I was very blind. And That's when my life started to decline. And then one day I began to cry. But deep inside of me I knew the reason why. I was living like a big lie. Like the devil who tries to be sly. And the Lord knows this isn't how I want to live or die. And so that day I prayed as I looked up to the sky. However I didn't even get a rely. and Then one day I met this guy. Who love the Lord as much as I. And he said to me with the Lord I will always be free. So together we praise On Bended Knees. To the father please hear my plea. And that's when I started to see. It was always walking with me. Sometimes I do feel lost. But no matter what I continue to carry my cross. And to be guided by the Holy Spirit Mighty Force. That gives me the power to stay on course. And from him I never want to be apart again or divorced. Because you are the Mighty God with all Existing Source.

Time for us to preach to the kids of today. Then maybe none of them would be locked away. And also show them the right way to pray. Because look at what's happening today. It's just like the Stevie Wonder song Love's in Need I love today. We need to do this before it's our time to go away.and to protect them from all the acts of prey. Another important thing is for us to listen to The Worst that they say. And to never let their relationship go sour or encourage them to go away. Because it could inspire that kid to disobey. So always showing them lots of love even when they disobey. Then they will respect you when you are old and gray. Having only kind things to say. So let's prepare the children because God's wrath is under way.no one knows when the good Lord is going to take them away. So today I will pray. That us all will be in Heaven someday.and now is the time to catch our children from being Castaways. you cannot see eye-to-eye. I meet them halfway. or no delay and make sure that they're okay. Talk to them when you take them out for a Sundae.

God is real and this is how I feel. time to stop playing games with my soul. because it's really getting old. For no one knows when they are going to die. but this is the truth and no lie. I'm sick and tired of playing head games. never wanting to take the blames. especially when I was insane. but now I can see with spiritual eyes. trying to be humble and spiritual wise. Because today I have nothing to hide. And I thank you Lord Jesus Christ. because truthfully you saved my life. thank you Jesus. believe me you are the reason. and I have decided to follow you. For you are the way, the life and the truth. and I truly do love you. Today my life is full of joy. Lord, you made me a happy boy. and it's you whom i'm living for. Because I've been constantly blessed since I opened up that door. That Door of Faith. In a spiritual life, spiritual safe. I must go out and spread the good news. to those who are blinded or being used. Because the Devil is a liar. and I'm sick and tired I live my life full of the wrong desires. Listen, it's time to grow up right. so that everyday will be a good night. always walking in the light. where the Heaven's spiritually is insight. For the Holy Spirit will make everything alright.

Today I remind myself I'm passing through this world. and to practice using good morals. this world is not where I belong. So day by day I will stay strong. as I patiently wait until my king calls me home. but in this world is where I prove my love and loyalty. to God almighty and all his royalty. I am here to spread the good news. so that people can win and not lose. To show people to be brave. so they can stop being sin's slaves. I wish we all could make it to God's kingdom. where it would be true freedom. Unfortunately that's not the case for the human race. in this world so many people are lost. when Jesus Christ paid the cost. the day he died on the cross. but they are in love with worldly things. I guess they forgot all about the mighty king. who made everything. and he's coming back soon. because the world is so out of tune. He's given the world lots of time. to completely renew their minds. but sadly people are walking the Earth spiritually blind and others are being so unkind. when Jesus said this is one of the signs of time. the world isn't going to get any better. and look at this crazy weather. Now ask yourself what really matters? Have you ever thought about the day you will die? will you be happy or will you cry? and only you know the reason why. so make that decision today before you die. remember Jesus said you are a love to die for. and he's constantly knocking at your door. Now that's the kind of love that I adore!

The Lord is My Inspiration

Fred woke up Sunday morning feeling so hurt. so Fred said to Wilma let's go to church. Wilma said okay, just let me and Pebbles get ready. and after that I'll call Barney and betty. so they went to church right down the street. and everyone they met was so kind and so sweet. and the preacher preached that morning. was all about God and all of his glory. and how God is your friend and will forgive you for your sins. and then all of a sudden Fred begins to cry. So Wilma asked him why? Fred told her I want to get saved before I die. and Barney heard everything and said. Come on Betty let's get saved with Fred. Both families got saved that night. because Fred woke up not feeling right. And when the preachers say them all. Fred was shouting down the hall. Thank you Jesus Lord Jesus Christ! Thank you for saving our lives. and then Wilma Said Fred, I love you. Then all of a sudden Fred yelled yabba dabba doo! Wilma I love you too! Meanwhile Betty told Barney I must confess. Barney you're the best! and after church they went out for dinner. when Fred blessed the food and said Thank You Jesus for forgiveness of our sins. For we were sinners. but with God in our life we are winners! because we are born again believers. For you are the greatest teacher!

How beautiful you are. Glowing Like the North Star. Your beauty lights up a whole world. Because God has created a gorgeous girl. To have your hand. Will make me a blessed man. And I want you to understand. I need you as part of my plan. When I first laid my eyes on you. Your beauty was too good to be true. I believe that God made you special. Because your beauty is so exceptional. I will give you the world, if the world was mine to give. But I can give you my heart as long as I live. Because your beauty is so unreal. It's like I'm in a dream. And You are my gorgeous Queen. And I wish I can buy you everything. And your personality is so Charming. Will you please be my darling? And your attitude is so lovely and warming. I want to be your best friend. Please understand. I need you as my Wonder Woman. Who can save my life. Will you be my lovely wife? And everything will be going all right. As I lead you into the light. Because our marriage will be blessed every day and night. Because we will be led by the light Jesus Christ. And I would thank God everyday. For guiding you my way!!

    I Want to Know What Love Is. Because for me it's like a big whiz. However, I definitely know how it feels. and so, I do have somewhat of an idea.but I want a love that's real. Not one who lies, cheat and steal. A love that knows how to heal. My heart when it's broken down. A love that will make me laugh like a clown. A love I can enjoy taking out on the town. Who catches my eyes when she puts on that revealing gown. Love is an intense feeling of deep affection. Love has taught me a great lesson. To always give the one in my life a good deed of attention and to always listen. And that way I can always win her love and affection. And in every situation always be her protection without a question. Love is God who is also Jesus. So it's true love can free us. From feeling any guilt conscious. Because love is honest. Love is holding on to all your promises. Love is respect, Quiet as it gets. Always having each other's back. And holding one another when one's sad or wepts. Even to respect each other when one gets upset. I know that true love does exist. And it's something that all humans really want on their wishlist. So it starts with God my Creator. Because there isn't no one or anything greater. Who knows my soul and fills me with emotions. And a true love with devotion.

Dear God, thank you for your Grace & mercy. And I feel like I'm not worthy. Because of my past. When I was living so fast. But you never gave up on me. Oh how I Praise You for Your Grace & Mercy. I want to continue to build up our relationship. For My Lord God only you I would fall down to worship. because you are worthy, and I thank you for your mercy. I can't express in words how much I love you. For you made my heart brand new. I wish everyone felt like me, because then the whole world will be set free. From a life of sin and Satan, do you know that the good Lord is waiting? For you to come and his loving arms. So he can protect you from any harm. He only wants the best for me and you, and cries when he sees us blue. Because he made me and you. We were created in the image of God almighty. So we are somebody! and when we obey his Commandments and do our job. Proving we are truly sons of God!!! And watch out for the devil for he's out to rob. Trying to steal your soul from you. Now you know what you got to do! Stand up strong with prayer and faith,so that you will be safe. Lord God I love you with all my heart, mind and soul let it be told! I have struck gold!

Sometimes I don't know what's wrong with me. Everybody is always looking at how I used to be. but I do believe. that I have lost my sanity. living in this Society. when it's Help that I need. So for now that's what I'll be searching. Because deep inside I'm still hurting. walking around always mad Lord have mercy. because For Your Love I'm thirsty. and I see that you are God almighty. my Lord all about you I do believe. and you are my destiny. because life with you I know I'll be free. living in eternity. you help me grow just like a tree. and I love you like nobody. and only you can heal my body. straightening me out when I'm naughty. And I thank you for all that you taught me. And in heaven you hold the keys. and you made everything and everybody. Lord help me please. and it's your love that I need. so I can start planning good seeds. life with you it's everlasting. and I know that you love me. and you know me to a Tee. and with you I have victory.

I will carry my cross, no matter the cost. Because you saved me when I was lost. today I will praise your name and I have no shame, well I'm not the same. For the better I'm starting to change. Today I will sing you a song, because you're my king who sits on the throne. Lord, you keep me strong. So that I can carry on. For you forgave me of my sins when I was wrong, so it's you in heaven where I belong. My home sweet home. Where I will never be alone. Today I will live by faith not by fear, thank you by wiping away all of my Tears, and all of the burdens and pain that I used to wear. Because you love me and care. And your love is always there. My Lord God you are everywhere, today I would love, because that's what we are made of. Loving my fellow man and woman, for it's a command and God's plan. And even my enemies I will try to love with my heart, for lack of Love Will Keep anyone body in the dark. That's why Jesus said love is important. of his commands, so love your fellow man and woman. In this world we're living in. Because if you don't you're committing sin. Today I will pray for you guiding us through this day, as I continue to carry my cross today.

 Nobody likes to be alone in this world. No man or woman, no boy or girl. No one under the sun. Because it's no fun. We Are Made for communication. And that's every person, nation and situation. Deep in the spirit of every person born. Needs a relationship with someone or their heart will be torn. And having a relationship with yourself is very important. So love yourself for certain. And also a relationship with others. Because we all are sisters and brothers. The most important relationship is one with God. And he said loving others is our job. Our souls cry out for love and affection. And that's without a question. And deep feelings of rejection, feeling, guilt and shame. Will play games on your brain. Driving some people insane. Or being a bruise will cause you so much pain. We try to cover our feelings hoping they will go away. But they get worse day by day. But we must love and forgive. Regardless of how bad you feel. We all have been hurt before. But that's no reason to start a war. However, God said revenge is mine. So continue to be kind. Because sooner or later you will be fine.

Our Father Who Art in Heaven. you are my god without a question. Father God I believe in you and this is my confession. My Lord, you have been so patient with me. Especially when I was blind and I could not see. That I'm the branch and you are the tree. And when I was hateful you still love me. I sometimes can't believe that I made it this far. My God, how wonderful you are. Just shining your love on me like a mighty star. I remember a time when you saved me from that burning fire. And anyone who says that you don't exist is a liar. Because I was trapped and I said God help me. And all the sudden the glasses start to break Lord you spared me. on that dark night. And now I know that you are the light. that can make everything all right. And there have been other times before. You gave me the strength to be stronger than Mighty Thor. You are my God who I love and adore. I thank you Jesus for knocking on my door. Because it's you who I want to live for. My heart you restored. And now it's time for me to stop looking back. And continue to put my life back on track. Lord, I Thank you for helping me in all of my Wars. And telling me that I am worth dying for. You are the lion of Judah. Who makes me want to scream hallelujah!!

    I want to thank you Father for the strength to wake up this morning. Your love is so strong and adoring. And also for my Lord Jesus Christ. Who died from me to have life. So I will pick up my cross and follow you Jesus. Because your blood and body will feed us. To keep us righteous and strong. singing and praying with worshiping songs. Life with him can never go wrong. Jesus is the bread of life. So we all need a relationship with him that's closer than a man and his wife. He's the wonderful Messiah. Who can baptize you with the Holy Ghost and with fire. Life with Jesus you will never go hungry again. Because he's The precious lamb who defeated sins. And whoever believes in him will never be thirsty. And every day I will pray for mercy. He is the light of the world who can show you how to have good morals. The light shines through the darkness. Because the light is Godless. Life is right when you believe in Jesus Christ, who will bless your life. Like when he assured the criminal on the cross. today you will be in Paradise. So Jesus is the holder of the keys to heaven for you and me.

    I will learn to forgive, as long as I live. Because if I don't, and I'm not doing God's Will. And he won't forgive me, so forgiving is the key. Because God wants us all in Perfect Harmony. Learning to forgive is very important, and that's for certain. when you don't forgive you will have some resentments in your head, that would leave you hostile and mad, now that's not good, that's bad. So don't stay mad at someone, try to forgive them for what they have done, and I know that it isn't no fun. But if you do you're obeying God's command, forgiving those the best you can. and if it's really hard to forgive someone, just remember what Jesus done. he prayed for them all the time, because not forgiving it's like a crime. So if you want a peaceful mind, forgive those who hurt you or made you act unkind. Because If you don't do it, it would rent space inside of your head, everything that person did or said. Take it from the Creator himself, not forgiving it's bad for your health. and learning to forgive, is the best way to live.

    We need to love our children. And then probably they will listen. do whatever we talkin about. Encouraging them when they have some doubt. Because they will be our leaders of tomorrow. So show some good morals to follow. We must love them all. As parents this is our call. To love and train them right. This way their future will be bright. Our world is getting out of control. And all of us are getting old. I pray to God that we can grab a hold. Of this world whose love has grown cold. All world leaders must pay attention to all of our children. so that none of them would line up in prison. Love is the key to about everything. And the more you give the more it will bring. God's love is our King. the one who created everything. you can learn all about him in the Bible. for he is my role model. And he loved us all and I think I know why. and I pray that you will find out before you die. however it's time to sow our children World Peace. So that none of them will be walking around like an evil Beast. Today we have so many mass shootings. and people are Wondering why and how. It's because there was no love for them when they was a child!!!

Sometimes I forget how blessed I am. Until I find myself in another jam. And I wonder where did I go wrong? I'm deep inside I feel like a ding dong. To tell you the truth God has been with me since my youth. I'm blessed in love by God the author. He is a magnificent father. How great is our God. Who's love and mercy keeps me standing at awed. and I do not care if people think I'm odd. call me a retard. for his Heavenly angels are my bodyguards. I will worship you for always and forever. And through the good times and through the better. are the light of this world. And a mentor and good teacher of good morals. I'm caught up in the Rapture of Your Love. And I thank you for all the spiritual gifts from up above. Lord I confess, thank you for my life you repossessed. From the evil one I'm so grateful and so impressed! For I am truly blessed. And I Faithfully do believe in you. Because all I've been through, I grew. There's no one like you. Today I'm crying tears of joy. Because you healed this bad boy. And now I can see. My God he was always right there for me. As a mighty tree. So I Pray On Bended Knees. To do your will. and to help others be free.

Thank you Jesus for saving a sinner like me. because without you I don't know where I will be. In this world I was so blind, sinning at the drop of a dime. Judging and cursing all the time. getting drunk every night, because I didn't feel right in the light. The devil had control over me, and I could not see, he was killing me slowly. I lost all of my morals I had, With a broken relationship with my Heavenly dad. I was a Lost Child, running and living wild. But deep in my heart, I want it out of the dark. This world is not my friend. Because it promotes sin. You will find some True Believers out there, who really do care. And they are everywhere! Today I have a relationship with my Lord Jesus Christ, Because he died for my life. I don't believe in religion, because they create divisions. With their strict traditions. Jesus Is My Religion, so that makes me a Christian. I believe in him, because he's the almighty I am who I say I am!! Jesus Is God and God is Jesus, he came to this world for so many reasons. One of the reasons is to love and he told us to love everybody. And not to be fighting! I will follow you my Lord Jesus Christ, Because he is the way, the truth and the life. So tell your children, friends, husband and wife.

Where would I go when I leave this earth? Why was I born with this birth? Is there a heaven and a hell? Are they a myth or are they real? And if they are, how could you tell? And why do people die? Making loved ones cry? Do you believe that we have a spirit? And if you do, would you cherish it? Keeping it healthy never sick. And why do people do evil things? If God made human beings. Because God is good all the time, so why do some people love to commit crimes? Why does it rain? Is the man upstairs in pain? And why do we need water to survive? If we don't have it we would die. And why do people eat animals? And why are we called mammals? And when did people start eating animal meat? When we have fruits and vegetables to eat. Why do people dream when they go to sleep? Are they strong or are they weak? Why do humans cover their bodies? Is it because we're naughty? And if we have a spirit why can't I see spiritual things? Like our almighty King? Who created us with a Spirit too. so I can tell him face to face,I love you !!!

The Lord is looking for you, if you're lost. He doesn't care where you're at or the cost. Because he wants you under his wings. with any problems that you bring. and he cares for you.Because he is alMighty king. who created everything. so my heart sings. because we've been redeemed. from all of our sins my friend. and it's important for us to understand. Life with him will never end. All you have to do is believe and you will see God almighty. when you leave this society. in Heavens you will see him. as he looks at your life on film. will you be ready for that time? because please don't be blind. just look at the sign of times. this world is beginning to unwind. Do you really know Jesus? Because here is the reason. He will say, on Judgment Day. I know you. And you respected my rules. so build a relationship with our lord Jesus christ. talking and praying to him for the rest of your life. be very careful not to get caught up and early things. like money, cars, Fame and diamond rings. Now tell me what does that all bring? when your soul will go to hell for everlasting. Please don't be insane. pray constantly and use your brain. and stop the pain.

There are people who like to live on the dark side. And they look like people who have already died. And they always wear the color black. It's the only color of clothes that they got. I mean what's up with that? They remind me of a black cat. Do they believe in God or the devil? Are they friendly or Rebels? it just blows my mind. That some people are so blind. I believe that somebody has taught them to be that way. To dress up in black clothes everyday. Some people say they are witches or and into Black Magic. Rumor Has It. Some people say they worship the devil. Are they living on that level? And they look lost and confused. Maybe they're getting abused? By you-know-who! The same one who's after me and you. How can they be so weak? When we all were made so unique. The color black sometimes represents death. Which means you have nothing left. However in heaven there are so many colors. And colors make you feel so much Fuller. Life is nothing to play with. Because life will be over and a swift. Who really wants to spend eternity in hell and in the Lake of Fire. Now to be honest, is that really your desire? If not, then put out that fire!

When I woke up this morning I began to pray. Thank you Lord for the strength to arise into another day. and in your presence is where I want to stay. Because you are the truth, the life and the way. and I pray to stay humble on his day in may. and to be filled with the Holy Spirit in this body of clay. And from your presence I never want to get away. because only you can make everything okay. and I want to thank you for forgiving me when I disobeyed. because from you my lord, I never want to be a castaway. but I want to be your protege. and so I will pick up my cross every day. and to celebrate my days just like a holiday. and it's you who I want to follow and obey. my God what else do I have to say. because I believe that your son has paid the ultimate pay. And in heaven I know in my mind I would be blown away. with the splendid things to see everyday. and so I do pray. please take my soul when I pass away. on that fateful day.

I want to be in God's Garden. where I won't turn rotten. a place of pure enjoyment and delight. and where everything will be alright. because daily we will see the light. as he shines so dazzling bright. This Garden is the place to be. With so many Splendid things to see. imagine no more sin. And happiness all over the land. and Everybody is your friend. and life here will never end. In this Garden little children can play with the lions, tigers and bears. without having a single care. and the lovest praise song will be singing so that everyone can hear it in the air. With people full of joy With No More Tears. And you will see Angels flying through the air. The Garden of God will have so many precious stones. in heaven you would never feel alone. because Paradise will be our new home. where the holy city will be pure gold. Just imagine yourself walking down this road. This place will be so beautiful with every ethnic race. and Finally we can see God's holy face with all of its Grace. Today I never want to sin. because I really want to go to heaven. so I pray that in God's Garden I will be when I pass away. that judgment day. because I won't have it any other way.

Love is the greatest word. That I ever heard. So make love your friend. Even if people don't understand. Love is the key even when your life hits a dead end. Commit your life to loving others. because we all are sisters and brothers. Take delight in doing it. Because it's a blessing to your spirit. Love is patient, love is kind. So do your best to love all the time. It's not boastful or jealous. That will lead you to being rebellious. and it isn't proud or rude. That can put you in a bad mood. However, love is kind. Helping others feel fine. Love is good. so spread some around your neighborhood. turning their frown into a smile. Picking up others when they are down. Love will bring joy in your life. Just like our Lord Jesus Christ. Love will bring you peace. Making you feel all your problems have deceased. Love is the spirit of God. So love is part of our job. Why do you think Jesus said you must love God with all your heart, soul ,mind and strength? It's because love is the greatest gift! And also to love your neighbour as yourself. Because love is important for your health. And no commandment is greater than these. So love others and God almighty will be well pleased!

The devil thinks he's slick, but all of his deadly tricks. And because he tricked Adam Eve, he thinks he's smarter than you and me. However, greater is he who lives in you and me. If you are a child of God almighty. And I want you to see, Jesus Christ paid the ultimate fee. Any left us with the Holy Spirit, who lives in me giving me peaceful feelings. So don't you let that devil outsmart you, I'll tell me what are you going to do? Fight a good fight, please do with all of your mic. As a child of God you will be alright see, if you just hold on tight. And don't let your heart be troubled, because the devil is out there trying to bust your bubble. Keep your spiritual eyes open wide, and remember greater is he that dwells inside. Be aware of the devil, that will take you down to his level. God has given us the weapons to defeat him and his Rebels. The devil is out to kill, steal and destroy, so don't let him take away all of your joy. Please be smart, stop living in the dark, because the Devil is a master at his art.now does that touch your heart?

Folks need to know the devil is real, and he's out there only to kill. He's out there trying to pretend to be your friend. And all he knows is to sin. Don't let him take away your place in Paradise, and here is some good advice. Fear God and Obey him, Then he'll see you listened when he plays back that film. The devil is out there to steal, and so now you know the deal, this is no joke this is real! Be careful how you live. And do your best to do God's will. For this isn't a game and it would be a shame. If God doesn't call your name. To come to Heaven up above in a new world full of love. Please don't do this to yourself, the only God knows how many days you have left. It's time to use your head. Because now is not the time to be spiritually dead. So pick up a bible and study it well, and pray to God to save you from going to hell. And pray to God to help you from going to hell, Remember the devil is a liar, who only has evil desires. And his permanent home is the Lake of Fire. It's Time my friend, because the world is about to end. and you have a choice to make, is it in heaven or will it be the lake, don't you know what's at stake? don't make that big mistake, For Heaven's Sake.

Today I feel all right. because I stay in the Lord's presence all night. I'm in love with the Lord Jesus christ. because he loves me and he gives me great advice. to better my life. He's the best who ever lived. The Lord is passionate and he loves to give. He was a rare Pearl. who came to save the world. From sin, death and despair. because he loved us so dear. even if we didn't care. He was always there. to rescue us from any nightmare. but the world was so blind. And some treated him unkind. because jealousy was on their mind. when he was God himself. the one who could keep the world in good health. but some people didn't get it. and if you mention his name they will have a fit. Maybe these people are really sick. but nevertheless Jesus was the best. and I must confess. He saved my life many times before. like when I was in a house fire. and I couldn't make it out the door. I remember saying God help me. because I was choking and the smoke was so heavy. and I could not see. But praise God the windows busting on their own. so I jumped from the upstairs window of our home. Today I understand for me God has a plan. and I thank him for letting me grow up to be a man. because of the fire that night. My brother lost his life. however he served the Lord with genuine love. so I know he's in heaven up above. and that makes me feel so nice. and I want to say thank you Jesus for saving my life!

Thank you Father God for loving me. and for your wonderful spirit that helps me to see. all your precious son Jesus Christ love has set me free. and I want to be a branch on your Holy tree. For you love me more than anybody in history. because you created me. Father God, I want to be a member of your family. for your love is strong like my mommy. And you knew us all when we were Unborn in our mother's belly. Now that's a mighty love so beautiful that we all can see. You sent your son as a living sacrifice for everyone who ever lived in this humanity. Thank you for showing that we all are worthy. to enter Heaven, a place with indescribable beauty. For this is my true destiny. This world has never been friendly. because it's filled with unholy. but not being a friend of this world is the key. And fearing God and obeying his Commandments is our duty. are the words from Solomon the wisest person to live in our society. And with God in Heaven is where I want to be. for eternity!

Today the Lord is the only way. I have to say. I tried doing my own will. But it always ended up going downhill. I also know that the Lord knows what's good for me. I saw pray that he helped me to see. that way I will believe. Today I will obey. my Lord commands. For that will help me be a blessed man. so that I can prosper all over the land. and I know that it's going to be a battle. So I'll try my best not to get unrattled. Today I follow Jesus christ. Because he's the one who saves lives. And no one can come to the father except through him. because he is him. He said to trust in God and to always trust in me, now can't you see? They are in perfect unity. The father, the son, and the Holy Spirit. And that's period. I feel for the unbelievers. so I will try to help them to be delivered. We need to continue to spread the good news of Jesus christ. because this is his will for us to try to save a life. So tell everyone, you and your wife. Jesus is the way, the truth and the life. He is the true vine who can also keep us in line. so that we can bear good fruit. because he is the mighty root.

The Lord is My Inspiration

Today is the day to live life in a different way. And to start listening to our father trying to obey. Before we are carried away I'm that special day. because we all want to live life feeling okay. So fear God and keep his Commandments is the best way. and in the next 24 hours is the time to put it on track. because when it's gone you can never get it back. and do remember the devil is always on the attack. so draw closer to God and He will draw closer to you. Even if you are a gentile or a Jew. He created me and you so talk to him whenever you are feeling blue. or when you don't know what to do. Don't you know he died for you? and his love is true. However, I know it's so easy to get caught up in this world we are living in. Everywhere you go there is sin. doing its best to get under your skin. so follow God almighty and you will always win. Now is the day to begin. For me I was so confused. And I was blind by the spirit of booze. I was living like a caged animal in a zoo. I didn't know what to do. I didn't know what to do. And no one knew what I was going through. Until the day I was put away. That's when I started to seriously pray. And I'm no better than anyone at all. I'm just a Wretched Man just like the apostle paul. But the path to a better way is through inheritance. the inherit of God's holy spirit!

A flower needs water or it would die.

It also needs attention and I think I know why.

because it needs love and affection.

For it to show some passion. to grow and glow its beauty.

So do your duty.

giving some tender, loving, and care.

and be always there.

Humans are the same way.

needing some TLC every single day.

I believe God is the reason why.

that we all need love or we will die.

In the Bible it says that God is love itself.

So love is good for your health.

keeping you away from death.

and God made everything, even the flowers.

with his unconditional love and his awesome powers.

and just like a flower we need lots of water. or we will die and that's no lie.

We also need some sun from up above.

shining down on us with God's love.

a flower will grow wild.

just like a child. if it doesn't have any TLC.

Actually, that includes everybody.

We all are in need of love everyday.

because love is the way.

to God's heart if you want to get far.

love is what God is and are.

shining down like the stars

My body is a temple, so I have to keep it simple. It's a place where God Spirit dwells, helping me from going to hell. And I must keep it clean, from all sinful desires if you know what I mean. So I need to start to treat it right, And let the Holy Spirit lead it to the light. With the good Lord it will be alright. So it's a win-win situation, and especially when I have temptations. And it's also good for me to learn meditation. And then I will feel Good Vibrations, With a loving sensation, Because the good Lord he is my inspiration. Many of us smoke cigarettes when we know all the effects. Are we that blind that we forgot? Smoking cigarettes will make you sick. So try your best to keep that Temple pure. Then you will receive blessings and that's for sure. Because you're living the right way, with the Holy Spirit dwelling in that body of clay. Prompting you with the right things to say, in these perilous times of today.

Jesus Is My Friend. who's always helping me to be a better man. and one day I will be with him in heaven. He died for my sins. man what a friend! He told me to have faith. and when I do I feel safe. Jesus is so good to me. It makes me and it feels so good to see. people praising our Lord almighty. praying for our society. happen though who do believe. be all that they can be. so that your life will be a happy story. praising God and giving him all the glory. because the good Lord will take away all of your worries. Thank you for being a friend. life with you would never end. and some people cannot understand. We are all part of your plan. because all they do is sin. they just can't comprehend. They think that Jesus was just a man. He is God almighty. who came to Earth in a body. to save this society. from the Devil himself. who is always trying to put us to death. Jesus Is My Friend. encouraging me again and again. to be a righteous man. for Jesus Christ is my friend.

Love is something we need everyday. and without it we would start to fade away. We all need it to survive. or your life would take a nosedive. don't be surprised. it's the most important commandment to do. so tell others I love you. to love someone. could be hard or lots of fun. so make it a habit of yours. to love everyone because it creates good morals. and who wants to have enemies. when love is the remedy. Love can complete your life. keeping you away from envy and strife. so love is right. Love is the light. that can shine or through the night. and having a feeling that everything will be alright. Love is a power. that can heal you in the darkest hour. chasing away the bad taste that can leave you sour. so send some love around. picking up others from the ground.For every human needs love in their soul. or their souls will grow cold. turning them into a miserable person. who always wanted to fight and always cursing. Desiring to kill or destroy or hate. who loves to debate. and they wonder why they can't get a date. From a lack of love this will be your fate. So please love for heaven's sake. before it's too late. Love is the answer. to run away from all of your life's cancers.

Why are you hard on yourself? Don't you know that it's bad for your health? I worry about you all the time. because not loving yourself it's not fine. give yourself a break for having sake. because you're losing your mind and I see all the signs. I don't like it when you cry. You are my best friend. and I will support you till the end. For my love is real. This is how I truly feel. and I will always be there for you. whatever you're going through. and I pray for you every night. because I love to see you living right. call me whenever you need me. and I will come running. to be right by your side. because being your friend gives me pride. so remember God Made You with his special hands. to be part of his plan. To tell people about his love all over the land. and to pray that people will understand. And how much he really does love us. For his love he wants to trust. So don't be hard on yourself friend. and do remember that God forgave you of all your sins. And life with him will never end. so be easy on yourself. and stay in God's wealth.

Love is taking a chance with your heart. Someone will cherish it, and not tear it apart. And remember it's a very important piece of art. So don't ever let anyone put it in the dark, Because your heart is who you really are. And having a good one would take you very far. Love is giving, that gives you a great feeling. Of love and happiness and healing. So you will always be willing, to help the one you love by giving. Love is being kind, especially when things get out of line, clearly, let them know that everything is going to be fine. With some patience and some time. Love is being truthful and not lying. They say that honesty is such a lonely word, and that's what I heard. But never the little less, do your best. To be truthful. Because when you do, you become more truthful. And the truth will set you free, then you can be all that you can be. And then people will see, the real love that you are holding. Love will take you to many places, and you will see different races, in Heaven with God's love and graces.

Why are we so easily influenced by others? When they're not even our fathers or mothers. Who always has the best intentions for us. Is it because we want to avoid a fuss? like the ones who have with our moms and dads. That will always leave us feeling mad. However be aware of who is influencing you. Because it's so easy to get in trouble hanging with the wrong crew. So be influenced by people with good Hearts. because you will see who they really are. And it would leave a mark. On you and your heart. But being influenced by the wrong people. Can leave you cold-hearted and what's the definition 2 of farmable definition tool phone number definition for vulnerable to evil. Living your life like a weasel. It can be so Lethal. so pick the good tree. not the bad tree, it's the key. and these are words from our Lord Almighty. Who is the true VIP! And don't get influenced by this corrupt world we're living in. Because it's so easy to be influenced by Sin. So who do you really want as your friend? What I would recommend. Just stick with people who are living right. You will be alright. And try to follow Jesus Christ. But he is the only one who can bless your life. So be influenced by our mighty king. Because he can do anything.

Lord forgive me for running away from you. for your love is too good to be true. I never had a love like this before. I love so strongly you went to war. and for me you died on the cross. finding me when I was lost. Your love is like nothing else. You taught me to love myself. I love you Lord with all my health. but you never gave up on me. when I was blind and I could not see. the dangers which were ahead. because numerous times I suppose have been dead. Your Love's like no other. more powerful than a loving mother. Because your love Lord today I'm free. and I can be all that I can be. as I grow strong like a mighty tree. Lord, I love you with all of my might. and I will follow you because you are the light. Thank you for dying for my sins. And now and forever you are my best friend. my life with you will never end. Today I will tell the whole wide world about you. because some people don't have a clue. and I'm not ashamed. to tell them about your holy name. because this isn't a game. I will praise your name Christ Jesus. for such reasons. You are the light of the world. who loves all the boys and girls. and all the people who believe in you. I thank you Lord for love, that's true. oh how I love you.

The Lord is My Inspiration

Today is the day. that the Lord has made. Let us rejoice and be glad in it. and to be grateful we're not sick. which can make us wicked. Today I will look up to the skies and say thank you jesus. because when I'm up there in heaven you are the reason. you die for my sins. so if I follow you my life will never again. you're more to me than my best friend. Some people find it hard for them to comprehend. so today I'm singing you a song. because your spirit helps me to stay strong. with courage to go on and on. life with you is where I belong. Because I know I will never be alone. With your guidance I can never go wrong. Today is the day I will meditate. How have you changed my fate. With your wonderful love that is so great. and I want to thank you for correcting me whenever I make a mistake. and you taught me not to hate. Today is the day. I want to stay under your wings. because with you I can do everything. and you are the Lord of the Lord the king of kings. And it's your name all of the heavens and earth will sing. you are the mighty Everlasting king. Today is the day I will follow you in every way!

Wake up people before it is too late. To enter Heaven through those Pearly Gates. and please don't get caught up in these worldly things. because heaven they will not bring. But it is time to start following the king. For he made everything. Including you and me. And he wants us to see. Heaven he made to live for eternity. some people just don't get it and they might call me an idiot. But just look at this world turned upside down. The devil is not playing around. He's trying to destroy everything in every town. wake up people open your eyes. and to keep your eyes on the prize. Where it would be so nice with pure goodness in Paradise. don't let this moment pass you by When you die. wake yourself up and give your life a jump. In the right direction and ask God if you have any questions. about living the right way. so that you can go to heaven on your Judgement Day.

People are unkind and so blind. they don't see the light or the sign of times. please trust in the Lord with all your heart. and do not let evilness put it in the dark. and never lose your faith. Also love is the only way. and he wants us to always pray. and hate is the devil's way. So tell me which one will you obey? the truth or the lie. So do the right thing before you die. so your loved ones will be happy when they say goodbye.

People wonder why we have to die. It's because Adam and Eve ate from the tree, Of knowledge of Good and Evil. And their genes are in all people. because we all are equal. So the Lord God took them out of paradise, because they disobeyed and that's not nice. And also to keep them away from the Tree of Life. Because if they ate it, they would have lived forever, so God banished them from the Garden of Eden for the better. It's sad to see loved ones passed away, because there are some things you want to say. To them before they went away. but fear God and obey his Commands, and then you will be permitted to enter the heavens. and this is everyone's Duty, to see heaven and all its beauty. But some people celebrate when their loved ones passes away, maybe because they know that they will be together someday. Or they know that their loved ones will be okay. But anyway. it's a destination we all must face, all of us from every race. So please love God and everyone, let him know you are grateful for all he has done. And you believe in Jesus Christ his son, and your soul will be won, When God's kingdom comes.

I will stop being hard on myself. because it's good for my health. and today I will start. to examine my head and my heart. who's been in the dark way too far. and it has become hard. and in my mind I don't want to be blind. I want to shine like a star and so I ask myself who you really are. And please don't put on a mask. just answer the question that I asked. because fixing his problem isn't a small task. so I will stop being hard on myself. because I love myself to death. I need to learn to forgive. if it's a peaceful life I want to live. and to have a good piece of mind. forgetting all of those bad times. and I know it's not easy to do. but I will start by forgiving me and forgiving you. and for father more. I will open up that door. to my almighty Lord. and ask him to restore my broken heart. because only he can fix this piece of art. so I will start being kind to myself. Because life with God is so full of wealth. And that's the best way to help myself. and I will learn to give. until I have nothing left and this is how I feel.

It's time to get your life right. So that you can have better nights. And Put your mind at ease. So that your soul would be pleased. because this world is going to die. And sin is the reason why. How much more abuse can she take? And sin is making her ache. She needs a break. And only God knows her fate. So live right before it's too late. Because Jesus warned us in the Bible. And the Bible is very reliable. Just look at the world today. Can't you see that she's going away. Bad weather, war and crimes. We are living in the end of times. Many diseases, Terrorist and Hate. Get right with God before it's too late. Man-made nuclear weapons of mass destruction. And he got the idea from the devil's instructions. That's not how God functions. God is love. Who's looking down from up above. Making sure that his children are alright. Every day and night. So I don't worry about anything. Because life with God is something. And I am just waiting for the king to take me home. To that special place where I belong. So hurry and repent before it's too late. So that you can enter Heaven's gate!

I used to wonder why I was born. and What I'm Living For. so I started reading the Bible. about the beginning of creation and about the disciples. And the story about Saul and how Christ changed his name to Paul. I learned the story about the rainbow. and I think that was so cool. God promised not to flood the Earth no matter what we do. The rainbow is a sign of his promise. and God never lies, he's honest. and I read about Jesus' mother Mary and joseph. and how the Mighty angel brought them closer. and I learned about abraham. a man of faith. Obeying God for whatever it takes. and then there was a man named david. whose heart was for the Lord he gave it. So the Lord made him king. and gave David many things. He was given the Holy Spirit. and expresses love for the Lord and his songs and lyrics. and Now I see I have a purpose in this life. It is to believe in the Lord and to live right. and that nobody's perfect. and that's for certain. and to be aware of the devil and his tricks. Who's the reason why we get sick. so I have a choice to make.to go to Heaven for Heaven's sake..

I want to soften my heart. because it's a wonderful piece of art. given it to me by God almighty. It's a Precious part of my soul. so I will protect it from growing cold. and from ever getting hurt. Which could turn me into a jerk. I will soften my heart. because God knows I don't want it in the dark. where it's sad and gloomy. making me act so moody. and no one will want to be my friend. And my heart will be weakened. Nobody wants to be around a cold-hearted person. who walks around angry, always cursing. I will soften my heart. and today I will start. by praying for my fellow man. given the best that I can. always trying to understand. every single human being. across the land. given a help hand. always trying to love somebody. and this whole society. Love is a beautiful thing. and the more you give. the more it will bring. so I will soften my heart. because it would take me far. in this life of mine. learning how to be kind. learning and giving all the time. whoever you are. try to live life with a softened heart!

Today I would love everybody. Maybe that's what's wrong with our society. or maybe there isn't enough love to go around and it's so hard to be found. or maybe people just don't have the time for love anymore. when in reality he's knocking at our door. and do you know love is where we all come from? So maybe that's why we all need some. Because without it we will begin to deteriorate. With a feeling that's not too great. So when it comes to love Don't underestimate. Love is something we must do. and I pray that it will see you through. of all your problems before you hit rock bottom. Love will keep your spirit strong. so when times are hard you can carry on. and love will have you singing love songs, all day long. Love is a remedy that will help you forgive all of the hurt in your past history. and I hope that people can see love is the key. to Heaven up there with the Lord almighty. because of a lack of love. I could only imagine how God feels up above. And I pray that the world would take this message clear. because love is in dire need everywhere. Why can't we stop hating each other? when God is our father, and we're sisters and brothers. And hating somebody because of their black or red or yellow or white. In God's eyes just isn't right. We are all precious in His sight. so love everyone and he'll see you living right. because love is the light.

The Lord is My Inspiration

God is great. and his love I do appreciate. God is everything. God is in the air. Yes, he is there. so he knows everything you say or do. and I know that is hard to believe but it's true. That's why he knows everything about me and you. Now does that make you happy? or make you blue. And if it does and what are you going to do. because he really does love you. He gave us a free choice to choose. whether we win or lose. you can do his will or your own. or you can do what's right or what's wrong. The choice is yours. Just remember the Lord is Knocking at Your door. and do you know what he's there for? because he wants to be your friend. with a friendship that would never end. Can you understand? He wants you to be part of his plan. so that he can take you to that special land. called heaven. isn't that nice. He's inviting you to Paradise. it's an offer you can't refuse. So what are you going to do? You have nothing to lose. your soul and so much more. because you refused to open up that door. So now in hell you live with the Devil, demons and death. That's what you will have left. and also the other lost souls. because you picked that heartache road.

Love is something I want. Let me get straight to the point. a genuine love of All kinds. that will keep my spirit and soul in line. but this is what I'm craving for. I love that others will adore. because I never want to go to war. or have a conflict with anyone. because it's no fun. I want to love that is true. even if it makes me feel blue. A love that's real. that I can feel. A feeling of peace. who put my mind at ease. having my Lord God well pleased. Love is the most important commandment of all. without love your world will fall. because it's our call. Love doesn't always feel good. however most of us think it should. But that's not the case. for the human race. Sometimes it feels like being slapped in the face. I will sow seeds of righteousness and love. as I patiently wait for the blessings from up above. I used to think love was a feeling of physical pleasure. but now I understand that's not the answer. It's so much more. it's what Jesus Christ died for. Love is something needed. In your soul and in your spirit. Love is that motion. that inspires me to a devotion. to my Lord Jesus christ. who died for my sins and for my life. today I would love with no strife

I want to thank God for the Holy Spirit gift. Which always gives me a Spiritual lift. Especially when I feel weak. He helps me stand strong on my own two feet. And he tells me what things to say. When things ain't going my way. He comes and saves the day. Also he assists me every time I pray. He is a comforter to my soul. And always teaching me how to be bold. Let it be told. Because the whole world needs to know. And he doesn't put on a show. He's a gentle Gentleman. Who tries to keep me from doing sin. So he's closer than a friend. And he has taught me so many things. Things that he heard from the King. And he's teaching me how to love. The kind of love from up above. And he's taught me how to forgive. So a peaceful life I will live. Also how it's good to give. and he's showing me how to be humble. so that pride won't make me crumble. Whenever I get in trouble. He always teaches me to be kind. Especially when things aren't fine. And everyone is being unkind. He gives me so much peace. That keeps me from that evil beast. And he gives me so much joy. Because he's showing me how to be a good boy. Thank you Holy Spirit!

It feels good to be a friend all the time. because I know that my love is genuine. and also it's for a lifetime. and my mission in life is to let my love shine. so bright and like the sunshine. as I keep striving to have a good time. Like drinking some happy wine. however I don't need any wine to feel fine. because too much of it will put me out of line. and that's not why I was designed. by God's purpose and divine. and I don't want to be left behind. or when it's my judgment time. because I'm really sick and tired of crying. or forced to be unkind. because it screwed up my mind. and so today I will take off my mask and let my love shine. and to be a branch on the Lord's grapevine. well I never want to live again like a filthy swine. Or giving anyone a hard time. I just want to be a true friend for my storyline. until the end of my time.

Love is something that I crave. And love is something that I always gave. with all of my heart. And lots of people tell me that's not smart. Maybe that's why at times I just fall apart. And only God can heal his precious work of art. and so today I tried to be smart. As I continue to search for my sweetheart. The one I can hold in the dark. And together and start a spark. Love is a spirit so you will never see or hear it.It takes over your mind. And also love is blind. Heavenly Father help me out. Because it's love I'm living without. Please send me one of your angels. For being alone can be so painful. I miss that good old loving feeling. That makes life worth living. learning to sacrifice and forgiving. Every day I will continue to pray. For true love to come my way. A love I can feel and kiss.is first on my wish list. And I understand to be careful what we wish for. And to be prepared for the one who comes walking through that door. Like the Israelites asking God for a king. And they had to accept everything. So today I'll try to stop the crave. Because love will sometimes make you a Slave!!

Love is the greatest gift to heal. And the more you give, the better you will live. Pure joy you will feel. Because love is real. Love you changes your life around. When it could be found. Picking you up when you are down. We need love to survive. And in order to stay alive. And living life without it you will slowly begin to die. And only God knows the reason why here he made us this way. So that we need each other each and every day. So love is the key for everybody in this Society. Animals need to be loved too. Just like me and you. 4 No one likes to feel blue. Love is a medicine for your heart and soul. It will make your life completely whole. Love is part of each one of us. Without it your heart will be crushed. Love is a must! Love is our creator and there's nothing greater. Then God the mighty one. And his precious son. We are to also love our enemies. Because love is a remedy. You must love and it's important. Love will bring your life goodness and Fortune. Because Jesus said love is the most important.

I want to say thank you to my Lord and Jesus christ. the true God who sacrificed his life. For me to make what's wrong right. and now I understand why it's so hard for me to be a good man. for this world is full of hate, all over the land. And I remember what Jesus said in the Bible warning me. That a sign of his time will be Wars and rumors of wars. Listen, this world has lost all of its morals. when I was a kid. Times weren't anything like this. for people stopped preaching to their kids about morals and respect. because for a fact. when I went to school and acted like a fool. the teacher will peddle me in front of all my peers. but it taught me to be respectful when an Elder was near. The world is changing and I'm not surprised. And now is the time to watch and observe and be wise. And one more thing I want to say. When it comes to God don't let anyone get in your way. for you are his pride and joy. Every man, Woman, girl or boy.

Sometimes I don't know how to think.

And my mind just goes blank. and I wonder is it because I'm weak? I wish I could go up to my mind to take a peek. Because it's peace that I'm trying to seek. Having a peaceful mind will help me feel so fine. Leaving all of my troubles behind. And then maybe I can shine. enjoying going out to dine. Enjoying a nice glass of wine. Just passing the time. Until It is time to unwind. This will be great for my mind. Making me feel okay especially when I lay down every single day. I want to say. Maybe then there's a better way. I don't know if there is one to follow. I don't want to keep hoping to hit the lotto. So I will pray tomorrow. That my mind has any sorrows. Because if it does I'll be hitting the bottle. And then I can't be a role model. So is peace that I'm looking for. Peace like I never had before. That's what I have been wanting more and more. So I will open up that door. To find what I've been looking for. the one who I truly adore. life with him it's not a bore please open up that door and take me for I'm Yours.

Sometimes life is hard. But don't let it tell you apart. Into a million pieces. All you have to do is to follow Jesus. Carrying that old heavy cross. because he is the way especially when your loss. And be careful in this world. that it won't take away all of your morals. Jesus is the only one not to sin. And look what this world did to the son of man! Can't you understand? This world isn't your friend. But Jesus is so try to follow him, and you will win.and when you pass away at the end. it would be time to celebrate with him in heaven. And the world wants you to be sad or mad when a loved one die or go away.however in heaven that would be a royal Feast every single day. Don't let this world control you. because it will have you feeling like you're living in a cage at the zoo. Or having you feeling lost in blue. so here's what we all need to do. ask Jesus to come into your life today. Because he's the truth, the life and the way. And what do you have to lose, are you confused? Don't be because the devil is out to use and abuse. Stop him in the name of Jesus. Because Jesus feeds us. With his spirit when he died on the cross. Forgiving us of our sins when we were lost. Because he paid the ultimate cost

Today in this world we're living in. is so full of evil and sin. and Today we are one day closer to the end. So tell me where do you stand? and what is your plan? Is it in heaven? in that paradise land? If yes then ask the Lord for his hand. because he is our friend. He knew you before your life began. and he wants you to take his free gift so that you can win. the right to go to heaven. and everybody born will have to go to court. so please give this some thought. God wants to give you a free gift of eternal life. where it would be so nice. with a city made of pure gold. and you would never get old. There will be so many different precious stones. With mansions that will be our homes. And there would be no more death. sorrow or pain. just look at all you got to gain! Thank God home will be with his people. As we worship together laughing and Mingle. and that this evening devil will be thrown into the lake of fire. with death and sin and all that is an evil empire. So tell me, where do you want to be? and all of eternity. because the world is dying. Please don't spend the rest of your life in the Lake of Fire crying.

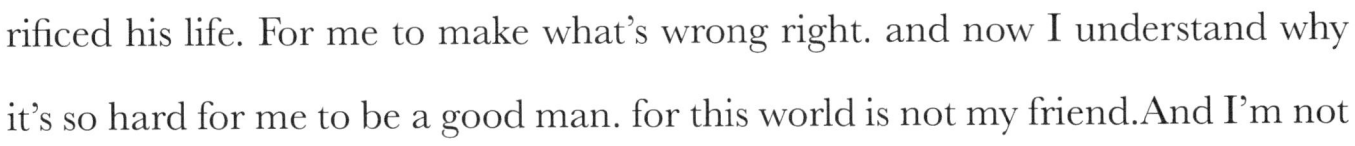

I want to say thank you to my Lord and Jesus christ. the true God who sacrificed his life. For me to make what's wrong right. and now I understand why it's so hard for me to be a good man. for this world is not my friend. And I'm not surprised. And now is the time to watch and observe and be wise. And one more thing I want to say. When it comes to God don't let anyone get in your way. for you are his pride and joy. Every man, Woman, girl or boy.

Some people love. and some people hate. So tell me which one is your trait? For love will help you with access through the heavenly gates. And hating will have you always waiting, to argue and debate. When you love you are obeying God's commandment which is great. for he will bless you because he does appreciate. however, when you do hate all you want to do is dictate. which is a bad trait. but when you love, it's easy for you to put on a righteous breastplate. However when you hate, People don't want to be around someone who likes to frustrate. And when you love it's easy for you to find a mate. that could eventually be your soulmate. but when you do hate. The devil has got you in prison as an inmate. But wait, it's not too late. to get your life straight. We are commanded by God not to hate. So we all are suppose to be teammates. So love others on earth and in Heaven we all can celebrate.

It's time for us all to be smart. and to always protect our hearts. because that's who we really are. We are living in an evil world. where so many have lost their morals. and God said do not love this world. and don't be sad about what's going on. just hold on to your faith and be strong. because a child of God in heaven is where you belong. so pay no attention to these fools. or their point of views. for this world is not your friend. and it's all coming to an end. because people have pride in their sins. The world is nothing like it used to be. just look around can't you see? People are unkind and so blind. they don't see the light or the sign of times. please trust in the Lord with all your heart. and do not let evilness put it in the dark. and never lose your faith. Also love is the only way. and he wants us to always pray. and hate is the devil's way. So tell me which one will you obey? the truth or the lie. So do the right thing before you die. so your loved ones will be happy when they say goodbye. It's time for us all to be smart. and to always protect our hearts. because that's who we really are. We are living in an evil world. where so many have lost their morals. and God said do not love this world. and don't be sad about what's going on. just hold on to your faith and be strong. because a child of God in heaven is where you belong. so pay no attention to these fools. or their point of views. for this world is not your friend. and it's all coming to an end. because people have pride in their sins. The world is nothing like it used to be. just look around can't you see? People are unkind and so blind. they don't see the light or the sign of times. please trust in the Lord with all your heart. and do not let evilness put it in the dark. and never lose your faith. Also love is the only way. and he wants us to always pray. and hate is the devil's way. So tell me which one will you obey? the truth or the lie. So do the right thing before you die. so your loved ones will be happy when they say goodbye.

Oh my Lord, I have a good feeling. Because of your love I'm healing. and I want to spread my lovin all around. Healing those who are down. with a smile instead of a frown. I want to expose the love of my Lord. because he is the mighty sword. whose words I adore. Do I need to say more? and he's knocking at your front door. He wants to come in and have an intimate relationship with you. So what are you going to do? and he can tell you everything because he wants you for he's our King. That can do anything. He can make your heart sing. He's good all the time. and he hates sin and crimes. and he wants to give you a free gift of eternity. and many more gifts if you truly believe. that no one goes to the father but only through him Jesus christ. or he's the first Resurrection to life. He is the Lord of Lord and king of kings. And all of creation is under his wings. He loves us so much that he gave us a free will. to decide how we are going to live. weather is to love or is whether to kill. However to love will be his will. And I am being for real.

Jesus you are the best. And I must confess. Nobody Loves Me Like You Do. A love so strong it's hard to believe it's true. You even loved me when I was breaking all of your rules. Because you knew I was confused. But you didn't give up on me. Even when I was blind and I could not see. A life of goodness you hold the key. I was living with so much bitterness. With severe depression I was serious. My heart was so broken. That I wanted to give up on coping. I just want to stay in the dark. So that no one can see me to continue to break my heart. And I will drink until I am beyond drunk. Yes my life was in a real big funk. More and more I sunk. However, I lost my freedom in prison. You Lord, you had all my attention. So I will read the Bible all the time. Asking myself how I could be so blind. I was living the wrong way. My priorities were so screwed up needless to say. I made money, my God. Sleeping with lots of girls was my job. I praise God for his Mercy. For truen love I've been searching. I know now that Jesus loves me and I wonder why. Because for so long I was a mean Spirit kind of guy. Today I followed Jesus Christ. Because he loves me and treats me nice . and every single day to the Lord I will pray. because he is the way. To Heaven on that special day. So I'm truly blessed that the Lord and I have a good relationship. And will be full of joy and I will make that trip!

Today I'm so sad that I want to cry. and I don't know the reason why. That I'm feeling this way inside. Sometimes I want to find a place to hide. Some might call it depression without a question. However, I'm sick and tired of being sick and tired. As I'm constantly losing all of my desires. Some would say that I'm sick, maybe that's why I Sometimes don't get it. but I do know that I want to get away. From having all of these dark days. And is getting to where I don't think no more.or is it because life is a bore? and I forgot what I'm living for. that I don't care about anything. but deep inside of me there is something.that's heavy on my mind. Saying to me that people today are more unkind. and many more are living in this world so blind. this world isn't what it used to be. And maybe that's what's been bothering me. so many truly godly people are passing away. It makes me wonder every day. Are we living at the end of the world? because it's so hard to find people living with good morals. And there are so many senseless crimes. Maybe this is the end of times! I mean how worse can it get? And now I see the reason why I'm sick. The Bible tells us that bad weather will be one of the signs and just look all around you please don't be blind. Is the end of times!!!

Please don't be a friend to this world. because it's not your boy or your girl. and all it wants to do is completely destroy your morals. this world is cursed with evil from the Devil. ever since he was kicked out of heaven he and his rebels. and now on Earth they're on our level. and we can't see demons. however, they are in all regions. The world is getting worse every day. just remember what Jesus had to say. and now Americans are full of lies, evil and Hate. and it seems like conversations always turn into debates. yep the world has gone wild. with these crazy things they're showing and teaching a child. because the devil is on the prowl. well he knows that God Almighty hears our prayers out loud. and if your friend to the world your enemy of God almighty. who wants to come and live in your body. and greater is he who lives in us than he that lives in this world. because we are all God's precious pearls. every man, woman, boy and girl.

The Lord is My Inspiration

I want to thank God Almighty. for my wonderful mommy. She was sweet as honey. I miss her tender love and care. A love that was so precious you couldn't find it anywhere. My mom was kind hearted. and she kept us well guarded. From anything that wasn't good. and she took us to church every time she could. Through you and dad we learned to have good morals. and to be a productive citizen in this world. Mom, you were unique and like no other. and you were an exceptional mother. and you love God so sincere. And I remember you praying with joys of tear. and I will wonder why you were crying at church. and I didn't know how to stop the hurt. but now I have grown to understand. That God forgives us of our sins. I never saw mom or dad. get angry or mad. about losing six children before their time. which can drive a person out of their mind. but you protected us like an angel from Up above. With a heart felt unconditional love. and I know you are in heaven as a citizen. teaching up there as they listen. Mom, your lovely presence I'm missing. but I understand God has got you on a mission. For he needed you up there. so he took you away from down here. Now I see it's all for the better. and someday we'll be together. Mighty and strong. as we praise God with a Victorious song. and I know with my heart up there is where I belong. my home sweet home. In a heavenly body. but for now I'm missing you Mommy.

I will hold onto God's promises. because in my heart I know that he is honest. And when I read the Bible and more each day. I want to follow Jesus because he is the way. Also the things he said would happen is happening today. I have to say. with the weather, hate, war and crime. we're getting closer to that time. When he's coming back. And I wonder how the world's going to act? And they see he is real. And every creature will bow down and kneel. to our Almighty King Every living and Dead thing. As the mighty Heaven starts to sing. Praising the Lord forever and ever. Because all things will get better. So today I will live my life not worried or sad. 4 this world is getting so bad. And all the Old Faithful Saints are leaving. So I'll hold on to my faith always believing. In the one who died for my sins. Trusting in him until life on Earth ends. In this world there is so much sorrow. Making some don't want to face tomorrow. So remember it is Jesus we must follow. Because with him we will be safe. So today I live by my faith!

I'm saved by your loving grace. for you have put a smile on my face. For your love is so strong, that it keeps me going on. In this world where there's lots of wrong. So I dedicate you this poem, And now in Heaven Is Where I Want to Belong. Thank you for your Holy Spirit you sent to me. Who helps me to see. Life in a different way. Comforting me everyday. With positive bold things to say. And I don't worry any more. Because it's you who I'm living for. And you will give all that I need. I thank you for my parents whom Planted good seeds. Inside of me. Lord You Are My everything. The Lord of lords and King of Kings! let the Heavens and earth sing. For I will lift my hands up high. Are you the reason why. I'm alive and born again. For you forgave me of all my sins. Thank you Lord for your grace. Because Heaven I can taste. I thank you Lord for not giving up on me. When I was blind and I could not see. The plans that you had for me. But your love has got me hooked. And I prayed for my name to be in your good book. The book of life. Will be so Heavily nice! And now I know what love is. For I am a child of his.